HAPPY WAY

INSPIRING STORIES FOR BRILLIANT KIDS

Melanie Mannerly

Copyright © 2024 Mannerly Melanie
All rights reserved. No part of this book may be reproduced or used in any manner without the prior written permission of the copyright owner, except for the use of brief quotations in a book review.
To request permission, contact the publisher at melanie@mannerlyme.com

This is a work of fiction. Names, characters, businesses, events, and incidents are the products of the author's imagination. Any resemblance to actual persons, living or dead, or events is coincidental.

First Paperback Edition January 2024

Web Page:
www.mannerlyme.com

HAPPY WAY SERIES

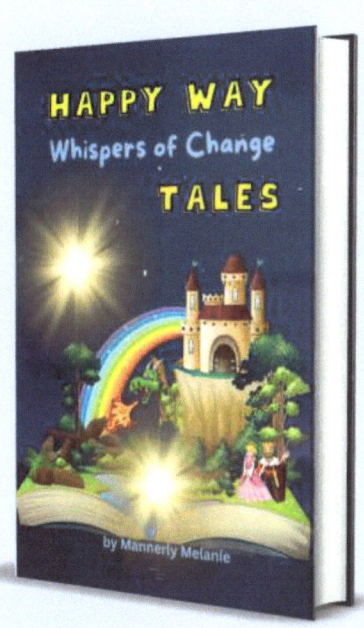

Visit my web page

Subscribe to my newsletter today and get gift, which, I must emphasize, holds no value for your kids.

www.MANNERLYME.com

Dear Reader,

I hope you and your child enjoyed the book and that it has brought you closer.

Would you be open to leaving a review on Amazon? I understand if you'd prefer not to, as your time is valuable. However, your review would be precious to me, as it would help me know what my readers appreciate and what they don't. I assure you that I read all the reviews and carefully consider them when writing the next book. Share a few words about your thoughts.

Thank you for considering this request.

I wish you continued success and all the best,

Melanie Mannerly
www.mannerlyme.com

TABLE OF CONTENT

- The Green Team: Little Heroes, Big Impact — 7
- Bianca's Musical Odyssey: How to Save Laughter — 17
- The Magic Tower: Be Worth of Trust — 24
- Archibald's Soul Adventure: Embracing Uniqueness — 32

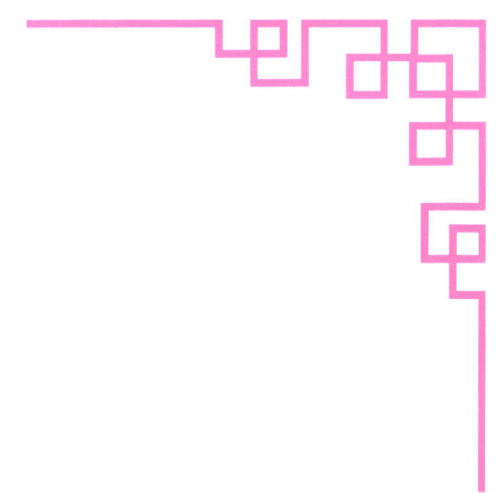

The Green Team: Little Heroes, Big Impact

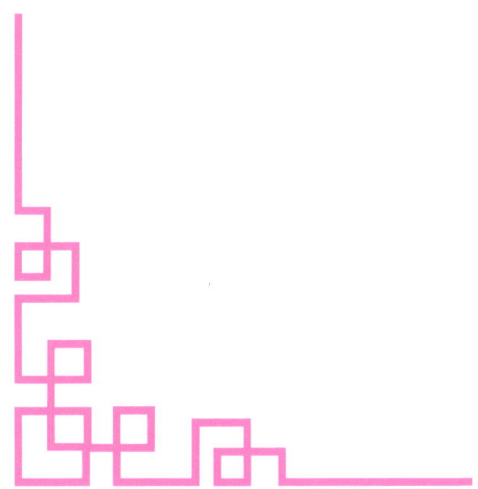

There was a beautiful lake near Brian's house, but something was terribly wrong. Suddenly, without any apparent reason, the water turned nasty and dirty. It emitted a disgusting smell, and no fish was swimming in it. No one knew why.

The lake had also become a dumping ground for garbage and old appliances. You could find all sorts of things there: fridges, cookers, car tires, glass and plastic bottles, old shoes, and even abandoned cars! It was absolutely disgusting!

Patrick and Brian used to play near the lake in their "secret place." While hiding inside a large, empty bush, they observed a pickup truck passing by and stopping beside the lake. Patrick and Brian remained quiet in the bush, spying outside to see what was happening. Two adults emerged from the truck's cabin, put on masks, and emptied large containers directly into the lake. The liquid was sticky and emitted a sickening odor. Once they finished, the individuals removed their masks, sat back in the cabin, and drove away. Patrick and Brian were petrified in the bush.

After a while, they jumped from the bush and hurriedly ran home. Patrick rushed into his house, slamming the door behind him. He was visibly agitated. His father asked him what was happening, and Patrick explained what he had witnessed near the lake. They immediately went to the location, accompanied by Brian and his father. Traces of the incident were still present on the ground. They promptly contacted the police, who investigated the matter and arrested the criminals responsible for poisoning the lake.

The residents were determined to recover their beautiful lake and take action. They organize the cleaning day to clean up the garbage. They worked together, filling two large trucks with all kinds of waste, including old refrigerators, cookers, and even abandoned cars.

They constructed their own water cleaning system to ensure the lake remained clean and safe. They planted various types of vegetation that naturally purified the water, including Hornwort, Watercress, and Reeds. These plants oxygenated the water and eliminated pollutants. After a few months, the water in the lake no longer emitted a disgusting smell. It became cleaner and clearer, attracting fish and birds.

The local people changed their living style and embraced ecology and green. They closed the plastic factory that produced plastic bottles, bags, toys, and more.

Canvas bags and willow baskets replaced plastic bags, homemade soaps, and shampoos gained popularity, and eco-friendly cleaning products became commonplace. Glass bottles replaced plastic ones, and wooden or cloth toys were preferred over plastic ones.

The villagers organized swap parties for toys, clothes, bags, and shoes to minimize waste. Instead of purchasing new items, they engaged in exchanges with one another. It allowed them to experience the joy of having "new" things without constantly being a new one.

They planted numerous trees around the lake and throughout the city. Children enthusiastically participated, digging small holes in their backyards and planting young saplings. They cared for the trees, watering them and witnessing their growth into tall, robust shade and clean air providers for all.

Many families began cultivating their own vegetables in their front yards and backyards. They intermixed the vegetables with beautiful flowers, creating a visually pleasing environment. Each family maintained a compost bin, depositing kitchen scraps and vegetable leftovers. This generated nutrient-rich soil for their gardens, enabling them to grow even more delicious vegetables.

The need for garbage collectors diminished significantly as everyone stopped littering, so garbage collection fees were unnecessary.

These actions produced a significant difference. Their shared home, Planet Earth, became cleaner, greener, and more beautiful.

Bianca's Musical Odyssey: How to Save Laughter

Once upon a time, a little girl named Bianca was in a magical land filled with talking animals and multicolored flowers. Bianca lived with her twelve brothers and sisters, and together, they faced a big challenge: a mischievous gnome had stolen all the laughter from their village. Without laughter, everyone felt sad and gloomy.

One day, Bianca discovered a magical book hidden in the attic of her house. As she opened the book, a small spark of light shot out, and the pages began to shine. The book contained a secret spell to bring back the stolen laughter, but it required the bravery and skills of a true hero.

Determined to help her family and friends, Bianca embarked on a thrilling journey. Along the way, she met Gertrude, a wise and quirky owl who became her trusty companion. Gertrude taught Bianca the power of friendship and encouraged her to discover her own unique talents.

In the heart of the enchanted forest, Bianca and Gertrude came across a mystical door guarded by a riddle. The carved words on the door read:

*I am taken from a mine,
and crafted with care.
Sparkling and precious,
I'm worn for all to stare.
What am I?*

Bianca carefully considered the words, searching for indications within the riddle. After a moment of pondering, her face lit up with understanding.

"The answer is a diamond!" Bianca exclaimed with excitement. "Diamonds are mined from the mine and carefully crafted into beautiful jewelry. They are known for their sparkling and precious qualities and are worn as jewelry." The mystical door swung open with the correct answer, allowing them to continue their courageous journey through the enchanted forest.

As Bianca and Gertrude made their way through the mischievous fairies' territory, the creatures couldn't resist playing pranks on the unsuspecting travelers.
The fairies conjured intricate mirror mazes, creating an illusion of infinite paths and reflections. Bianca and Gertrude found themselves trapped, unsure of which way to go. Bianca suggested they use a small enchanted compass she had tucked away in her pocket. The object shows the direction to follow, they were able to identify the real path and navigate through the maze with ease.

As they continued their adventure, Bianca found a door to a magical cave. They discovered a piano, a guitar, and many other instruments inside. Bianca read in the magic book that to break the spell and bring back the laughter; she needed to play a joyful tune that would touch the hearts of everyone in the village.

With Gertrude's guidance, Bianca practiced day and night, playing the piano and strumming the guitar with passion and determination.

Finally, the day of the grand performance arrived. Bianca stood before the entire village, her heart racing with excitement. As she played a magical melody on the piano, the villagers smiled, laughed, and danced. The stolen laughter returned, filling the air with joy and harmony. Bianca had become a true hero, using her talents and competence to save the village and bring back happiness.

Whenever she looked up at the night sky, she would see Gertrude, the owl who had become her lifelong friend and mentor, watching over her with a twinkle in her wise, sparkling eyes.

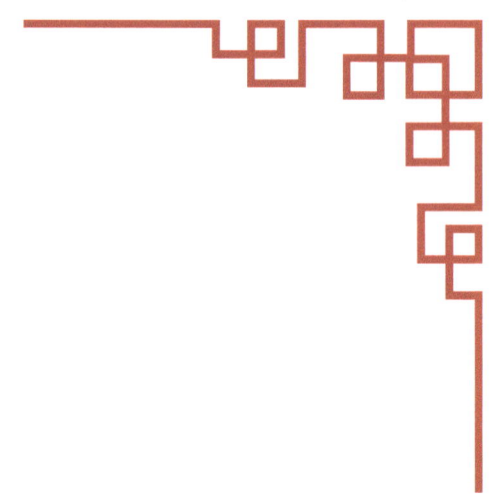

"The Magic Tower: Be Worth of Trust"

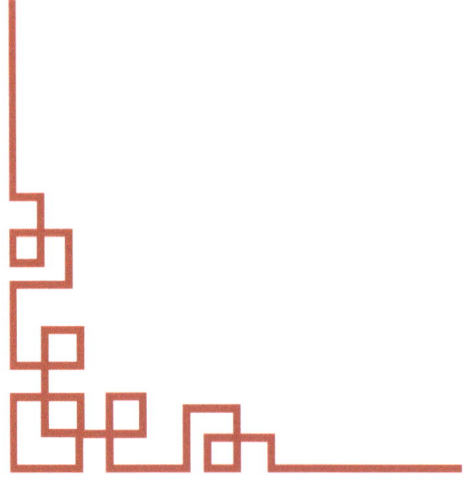

Once upon a time, in a tiny village, two brave kids named Alex and Bellatrix made an exciting discovery. Deep in the woods, they stumbled upon an ancient, mysterious tower said to hold magical treasures. But beware! It was guarded by a mischievous forest spirit that locked anyone who entered and never let them out.

One moonlit night, Alex and Bellatrix ventured into the woods armed with flashlights and curiosity, determined to explore the tower together. As they approached the towering structure, the forest fell eerily silent.

Climbing the creaky stairs, they felt a mix of excitement and fear. Suddenly, the door slammed shut behind them, trapping them inside. The tower seemed to come alive, shifting its passages, leaving them lost!

Ha Ha Ha Ha Ha Ha

Trying to find their way out, they felt like they were in a maze, going in circles. They could hear the forest spirit's mischievous laughter. But Alex and Bellatrix refused to give up; they had to keep going and try to find a way out.

After a while, they entered a room with a table in the middle. A tempting donut filled with cream and sprinkled with chocolate sat on the table. Next to it was a note that said, "If you eat the donut, you will find a way out, but only one can eat." Alex and Bellatrix looked at each other, worried about what to do. One could save themselves by eating the donut, but the other would remain trapped forever.

Alex had an idea and said, "Let's cut it in half, and each eats half." So they did, savoring the soft, sweet treat. Suddenly, they heard a loud noise, "BRUM, BAM," and the wall behind the table opened up, leading them into the next room.

In this room, a christal lamp hangs from the ceiling. They heard many whispered voices, saying, "If you reveal your friend's secret, we will let you out, but only one can go free." The voices echoed all around them. Alex and Bellatrix knew they wouldn't betray each other. They covered their ears with their fingers to avoid temptation, and the voices disappeared.

But then, the floor beneath Bellatrix's feet opened, and she fell into a dark hall. Alex was still in the room. Bellatrix called out to Alex, and he reassured her that he would find a way to rescue her.

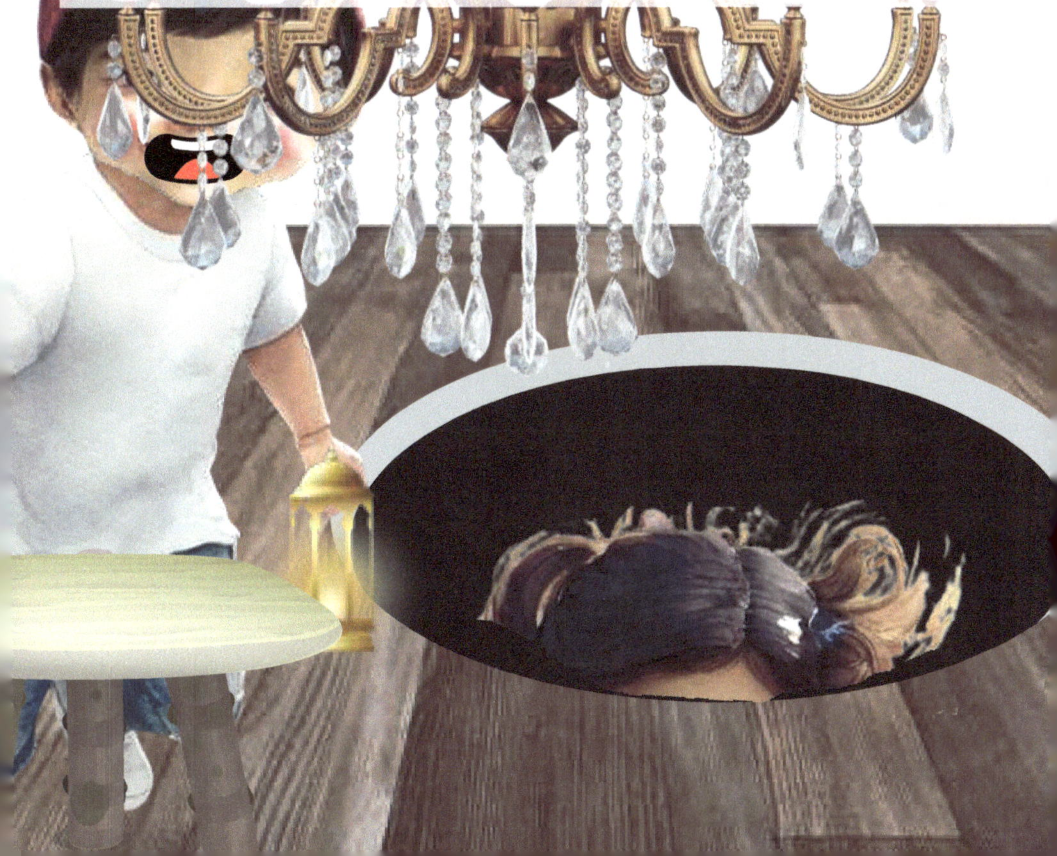

At that moment, a small, green-skinned man with red eyes appeared before Alex. He said, "Don't be afraid, young one. I can give you a bag full of diamonds and gold. You will be rich and have everything you desire for all your life, only if you leave your friend behind." Alex was tempted but quickly replied, "No, I want to save her. Help me get her out of the hole." The green man got angry and caused the floor to collapse, making Alex fall into the hole with Bellatrix.

In the dark, hot hole, they found a doorknob and opened the door to a room. There, they saw a magical bottle of water on the table. Alex and Bellatrix were thirsty, but the label said, "Only one can drink from this bottle." Bellatrix had an idea and said, "I'll leave the room, so you can drink first. Then, I'll come back, and you can leave the room, so I can drink. But if the door opens while you're drinking, call me so I can escape with you. Will you promise?"

Only one can drink from this bottle.

"Yes, I promise," said Alex. She left the room and waited anxiously behind the door. Suddenly, Alex called out, "Bellatrixe, run!" She quickly opened the door, rushed into the room, took Alex's hand, and ran out because while Alex was drinking, one wall disappeared, revealing the way out to the forest.

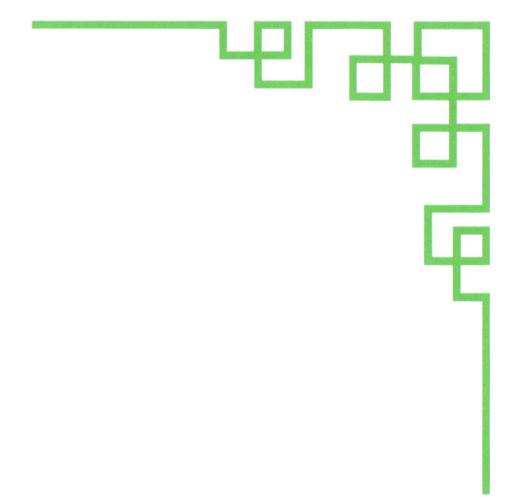

Archibald's Soul Adventure: Embracing Uniqueness

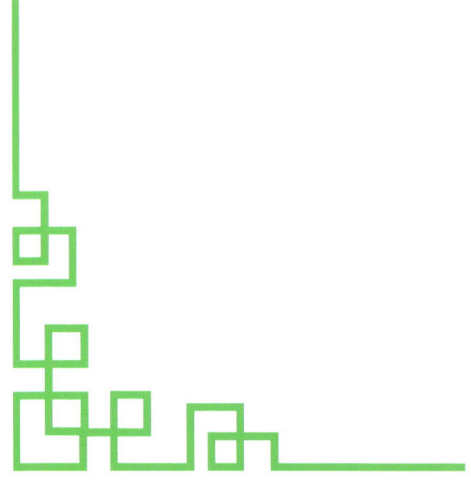

Once upon a time, two brothers named Griffin and Archibald lived in a deep, dark forest. They loved to play and practice to become brave hunters. In the deep, dark forest, towering ancient trees formed a thick roof above Griffin and Archibald. The sunlight struggled to penetrate the thick foliage, dappling patterns on the forest floor. With handmade spears skillfully crafted from the forest's resources, they honed their hunting skills.

Griffin mentored Archibald's precision aiming while Archibald showcased agile footwork. They were an exceptional team, each complementing the other's strengths. One day, they stumbled upon a crystal-clear stream, its vibrant blue reflecting the sky. They sensed the unspoiled harmony uniting all life as they drank from it.
In those days, the land, the water, and the sky belonged to everyone—humans and animals alike. The only thing a person indeed possessed was their soul.

One fateful day, as Griffin was wandering through the forest, he encountered the evil Crackerjack. Crackerjack had a strange power—he could hypnotize people!

He used his magic to hypnotize Griffin and whispered an evil plan into his ear. The goal was to steal Archibald's soul! Griffin did not want to and promised to give him the soul of a dear. But Crackerjack wants a unique and special Archibald soul. Griffin, hypnotized, could not oppose that command. Then, with a sneaky smile, Crackerjack disappeared into the shadows.

When Griffin returned to Archibald, he felt odd but couldn't quite remember what happened. Suddenly, he noticed something extraordinary—he could see his brother's soul! It was like a glowing ball of light within Archibald. Griffin stretched out his hand, trying to grasp the soul. Still, it was elusive, changing shape and slipping away like a fluttering butterfly.

Eventually, it soared up into the sky. Without the soul, Archibald's body lay still on the forest floor, lifeless. You see, it's the soul that keeps the body alive. When Griffin realized what he had done, he fell to his knees, tears streaming down his cheeks. He cried out in despair.

Unrevealed to Griffin, the evil Crackerjack had been listening from afar. Surprisingly, he felt a tinge of regret for his wicked actions. Crackerjack called out to Archibald's unique soul, asking it to return to its body. As if by magic, Archibald opened his eyes, alive once more!

Griffin and Archibald embraced tightly, tears of joy in their eyes. They were reunited, and it was a moment of immense happiness.

www.ingramcontent.com/pod-product-compliance
Lightning Source LLC
Chambersburg PA
CBHW041605220426
43661CB00015B/1191